MUNICH
RESTAURANT
GUIDE 2018

RESTAURANTS, BARS & CAFES

★★★★★

The Most Positively
Reviewed and Recommended
Restaurants in the City

MUNICH RESTAURANT GUIDE 2018
Best Rated Restaurants in Munich, Germany

© Timothy F. Gottlieb, 2018
© E.G.P. Editorial, 2018

Printed in USA.

ISBN-13: 978-1545461921
ISBN-10: 1545461929

Copyright © 2018
All rights reserved.

MUNICH RESTAURANTS 2018
The Most Recommended Restaurants in Munich

This directory is dedicated to Munich Business Owners and Managers who provide the experience that the locals and tourists enjoy. Thanks you very much for all that you do and thank for being the "People Choice".

Thanks to everyone that posts their reviews online and the amazing reviews sites that make our life easier.

The places listed in this book are the most positively reviewed and recommended by locals and travelers from around the world.

Thank you for your time and enjoy the directory that is designed with locals and tourist in mind!

TOP 500
RESTAURANTS
Ranked from #1 to #500

Munich Restaurant Guide 2018 / Restaurants, Bars & Cafés

#1
Royal Kebabhaus
Cuisines: Kebab
Average price: Inexpensive
Address: Arnulfstr. 5 80336 Munich
Phone: +49 89 23542924

#2
Sababa
Cuisines: Oriental
Average price: Inexpensive
Address: Westenriederstr. 9 80331 Munich
Phone: +49 89 23237881

#3
Schmalznudel Frischhut
Cuisines: Café, Bakery
Average price: Modest
Address: Prälat-Zistl-Str. 8 80331 Munich
Phone: +49 89 268237

#4
Ringlers
Cuisines: Fast Food, Sandwiches, Ice Cream
Average price: Inexpensive
Address: Sendlinger Str. 45 80331 Munich
Phone: +49 89 265549

#5
Ennstaler Stubn
Cuisines: Bavarian, Austrian
Average price: Inexpensive
Address: Reifenstuelstr. 1 80469 Munich
Phone: +49 89 46135737

#6
Upper Eat Side
Cuisines: German, Tapas
Average price: Expensive
Address: Werinherstr. 15 81541 Munich
Phone: +49 89 39292689

#7
Nur Einmal Leben
Cuisines: Greek, Mediterranean
Average price: Modest
Address: Riesenfeldstr. 72 80809 Munich
Phone: +49 89 35396563

#8
Manam
Cuisines: Thai
Average price: Modest
Address: Rosenheimerstr. 34 81669 Munich
Phone: +49 176 99029311

#9
DuDu
Cuisines: Vietnamese
Average price: Modest
Address: Augsburgerstr. 1 80337 Munich
Phone: +49 89 12286480

#10
Anh Thu
Cuisines: Vietnamese
Average price: Expensive
Address: Kurfürstenstr. 31 80801 Munich
Phone: +49 89 27374117

#11
Café Centro
Cuisines: Italian, Café
Average price: Inexpensive
Address: Tegernseer Platz 1 81541 Munich
Phone: +49 89 20047101

#12
Augustiner Bräustuben
Cuisines: German, Bavarian
Average price: Modest
Address: Landsbergerstr. 19 80339 Munich
Phone: +49 89 507047

#13
Da Rosario
Cuisines: Pizza, Italian, Mediterranean
Average price: Modest
Address: Schönfeldstr. 24 80539 Munich
Phone: +49 89 24242682

#14
Salt Restaurant
Cuisines: International
Average price: Expensive
Address: Rundfunkplatz 4 80335 Munich
Phone: +49 89 89083695

#15
Gasthaus Weinbauer
Cuisines: Bavarian
Average price: Modest
Address: Fendstr. 5 80802 Munich
Phone: +49 89 38887102

#16
Jasmin Asia Cuisine
Cuisines: Vietnamese, Asian Fusion
Average price: Modest
Address: Lindwurmstr. 167 80337 Munich
Phone: +49 89 76775712

#17
Gaststätte Lindengarten
Cuisines: German, Beer Garden
Average price: Modest
Address: Solalindenstr. 50 81825 Munich
Phone: +49 89 4309178

#18
Tantris Restaurant
Cuisines: International
Average price: Exclusive
Address: Johann-Fichte-Str. 7 80805 Munich
Phone: +49 89 3619590

#19
Champor
Cuisines: Malaysian
Average price: Expensive
Address: Warthe Str. 5 81927 Munich
Phone: +49 89 99317764

#20
Restaurant Zauberberg
Cuisines: European
Average price: Expensive
Address: Hedwigstr. 14 80636 Munich
Phone: +49 89 18999178

#21
Das Gaumenspiel
Cuisines: Café, Breakfast & Brunch
Average price: Modest
Address: Haimhauserstr. 11 80802 Munich
Phone: +49 89 33038633

#22
Augustiner-Keller
Cuisines: Bavarian
Average price: Modest
Address: Arnulfstr. 52 80335 Munich
Phone: +49 89 594393

#23
Frontküche
Cuisines: Bavarian
Average price: Inexpensive
Address: Theresienstr. 93 80333 Munich
Phone: +49 176 61660264

#24
Broeding
Cuisines: German, European
Average price: Expensive
Address: Schulstr. 9 80634 Munich
Phone: +49 89 164238

#25
Gasthaus Isarthor
Cuisines: Bavarian
Average price: Modest
Address: Kanalstr. 2 80538 Munich
Phone: +49 89 227753

#26
Bamyan Narges
Cuisines: Afghan
Average price: Modest
Address: Hans-Sachs-Str. 3 80469 Munich
Phone: +49 89 23888878

#27
Zum Alten Kreuz
Cuisines: German, Bavarian
Average price: Modest
Address: Falkenstr. 23 81541 Munich
Phone: +49 89 65308091

#28
Cooperativa
Cuisines: Mediterranean
Average price: Modest
Address: Jahnstr. 35 80469 Munich
Phone: +49 89 20207620

#29
Goldmarie
Cuisines: German, Austrian
Average price: Modest
Address: Schmellerstr. 23 80337 Munich
Phone: +49 89 51669272

#30
Kao Kao
Cuisines: Asian Fusion, Wine Bar, Thai
Average price: Expensive
Address: Tulbeckstr. 9 80339 Munich
Phone: +49 89 505400

#31
Wirtshaus in der Au
Cuisines: German
Average price: Modest
Address: Lilienstr. 51 81669 Munich
Phone: +49 89 4481400

#33
Take Don
Cuisines: Japanese
Average price: Modest
Address: Erzgiessereistr. 32 80335 Munich
Phone: +49 89 23710781

#32
Opatija Am Alten Peter
Cuisines: Mediterranean
Average price: Inexpensive
Address: Rindermarkt 2 80331 Munich
Phone: +49 89 23231995

#34
Mitani
Cuisines: Japanese
Average price: Expensive
Address: Rablstr. 45 81669 Munich
Phone: +49 89 4489526

#35
Gaststätte Zum Brünnstein
Cuisines: German
Average price: Inexpensive
Address: Elsässer Str. 36 81667 Munich
Phone: +49 89 4482429

#36
Hamburgerei
Cuisines: Burgers, Fast Food
Average price: Modest
Address: Brienner Str. 49 80333 Munich
Phone: +49 89 20092018

#37
Tramin
Cuisines: European, Mediterranean
Average price: Exclusive
Address: Lothringer Str. 7 81667 Munich
Phone: +49 89 44454090

#38
Andechser am Dom
Cuisines: German
Average price: Modest
Address: Weinstr. 7a 80333 Munich
Phone: +49 89 298481

#39
Franzz
Cuisines: Gastropub, German, Beer Garden
Average price: Modest
Address: Bäckerstr. 89 81241 Munich
Phone: +49 89 63876838

#40
Mimi Asia
Cuisines: Vietnamese
Average price: Inexpensive
Address: Westendstr. 148 80339 Munich
Phone: +49 89 50077062

#41
Belicious
Cuisines: Burgers
Average price: Modest
Address: Pariser Str. 34 81667 Munich
Phone: +49 89 62502878

#42
Takumi
Cuisines: Japanese
Average price: Modest
Address: Heßstr.71 80798 Munich
Phone: +49 89 528599

#43
Restaurant am Chinesischen Turm
Cuisines: German, Beer Garden
Average price: Modest
Address: Englischer Garten 3 80538 Munich
Phone: +49 89 3838730

#44
The Grill
Cuisines: Lounge, European, Steakhouse
Average price: Expensive
Address: Lenbachplatz 8 80333 Munich
Phone: +49 89 45205950

#45
Gartensalon
Cuisines: Café
Average price: Modest
Address: Türkenstr. 90 80799 Munich
Phone: +49 89 28778604

#46
Trinacria Der Sizilianer
Cuisines: Italian
Average price: Modest
Address: Balanstr. 25 81669 Munich
Phone: +49 89 45479084

#47
Ruff's Burger
Cuisines: Burgers
Average price: Modest
Address: Occamstr. 4 80802 Munich
Phone: +49 89 12598616

#48
Savanna
Cuisines: African, Steakhouse
Average price: Modest
Address: Maistr. 63 80337 Munich
Phone: +49 89 53906363

#49
La Brasserie
Cuisines: French
Average price: Expensive
Address: Hirschgartenallee 41 80639 Munich
Phone: +49 89 174232

#50
Makassar
Cuisines: French, Bar, Cajun, Creole
Average price: Modest
Address: Dreimühlenstr. 25 80469 Munich
Phone: +49 89 776959

#51
Condesa
Cuisines: Mexican
Average price: Inexpensive
Address: Münchner Freiheit Nr. 6 80802 Munich
Phone: +49 176 20227136

#52
Waldfee
Cuisines: Bar, German, Austrian
Average price: Modest
Address: Occamstr. 13 80802 Munich
Phone: +49 89 84008310

#53
Hofbräuhaus
Cuisines: German, Bavarian
Average price: Modest
Address: Platzl 9 80331 Munich
Phone: +49 89 2901360

#54
Nage & Sauge
Cuisines: German, Bar, International
Average price: Modest
Address: Mariannenstr. 2 80538 Munich
Phone: +49 89 298803

#55
Cocoon
Cuisines: European, German
Average price: Expensive
Address: Christophstr. 3 80538 Munich
Phone: +49 89 25541966

#56
Mezzodi
Cuisines: Italian, Café
Average price: Modest
Address: Steinstr. 57 81667 Munich
Phone: +49 89 484950

#57
Shane's Restaurant
Cuisines: European, Asian Fusion, Cocktail Bar
Average price: Expensive
Address: Geyerstr. 52 80469 Munich
Phone: +49 89 74646820

#58
Leib und Seele
Cuisines: German
Average price: Modest
Address: Oettingenstr. 36 80538 Munich
Phone: +49 89 21028899

#59
Zwickl
Cuisines: Bavarian, Lounge
Average price: Modest
Address: Dreifaltigkeitsplatz 2 80331 Munich
Phone: +49 89 46228833

#60
Tira Tardi
Cuisines: Italian
Average price: Expensive
Address: Kurfürstenstr. 41 80801 Munich
Phone: +49 89 27774455

#61
Landersdorfer & Innerhofer
Cuisines: German
Average price: Expensive
Address: Hackenstr. 6-8 80331 Munich
Phone: +49 89 26018637

#62
Rusticana
Cuisines: Barbeque, Steakhouse
Average price: Expensive
Address: Grillparzerstr. 5 81675 Munich
Phone: +49 89 4703887

#63
Josefa
Cuisines: Café, Cocktail Bar
Average price: Modest
Address: Westendstr. 29 80339 Munich
Phone: +49 89 28979183

#64
Königshof Restaurant
Cuisines: European
Average price: Exclusive
Address: Karlsplatz 25 80335 Munich
Phone: +49 4908 955136-0

#65
Olympia Alm
Cuisines: Beer Garden
Average price: Modest
Address: Martin-Luther-King Weg 8
80809 Munich
Phone: +49 89 3009924

#66
Harlachinger Jagdschlössl
Cuisines: Bavarian, German
Average price: Modest
Address: Geiselgasteigstr. 153 81545 Munich
Phone: +49 89 30906760

#67
Wirtshaus Zum Straubinger
Cuisines: Beer Garden, Gastropub, Bavarian
Average price: Expensive
Address: Blumenstr. 5 80331 Munich
Phone: +49 89 232383-0

#68
Oliveto
Cuisines: Italian, Mediterranean
Average price: Modest
Address: Häberlstr. 9 80337 Munich
Phone: +49 89 59993913

#69
Preysinggarten
Cuisines: Mediterranean, Café
Average price: Modest
Address: Preysingstr. 69 81667 Munich
Phone: +49 89 6886722

#70
Banyan
Cuisines: Vietnamese
Average price: Expensive
Address: Goethestr. 68 80336 Munich
Phone: +49 89 5309321

#71
Weisses Bräuhaus
Cuisines: Bavarian, German, Brewerie
Average price: Modest
Address: Tal 7 80331 Munich
Phone: +49 89 290138-0

#72
Pizzeria Rosso
Cuisines: Pizza
Average price: Modest
Address: Amalienstr. 45 80799 Munich
Phone: +49 89 27375653

#73
J-Bar
Cuisines: Japanese
Average price: Modest
Address: Maistr. 28 80337 Munich
Phone: +49 89 51469983

#74
Marbella
Cuisines: Spanish, Tapas
Average price: Modest
Address: Horemansstr. 30 80636 Munich
Phone: +49 89 12779753

#75
Natraj Indisches Restaurant
Cuisines: Indian
Average price: Modest
Address: Nymphenburger Str. 26
80335 Munich
Phone: +49 89 12001262

#76
Ratskeller
Cuisines: Wine Bar, German, Brewerie
Average price: Modest
Address: Marienplatz 8 80331 Munich
Phone: +49 89 2199890

#77
Le Barestovino
Cuisines: French
Average price: Expensive
Address: Thierschstr. 35 80538 Munich
Phone: +49 89 23708355

#78
Pacific-Times
Cuisines: Cocktail Bar, International
Average price: Expensive
Address: Baaderstr. 28 80469 Munich
Phone: +49 89 20239470

#79
Restaurant Hu
Cuisines: Chinese
Average price: Modest
Address: Boschetsrieder Str. 72
81379 Munich
Phone: +49 89 72448490

#80
Restaurant Gut Nederling
Cuisines: Austrian, German
Average price: Modest
Address: Nederlingerstr. 78 80638 Munich
Phone: +49 89 14338874

#81
Wein Cantina
Cuisines: Winery, International, Venues, Event Space
Average price: Expensive
Address: Elsässerstr. 23 81667 Munich
Phone: +49 89 44419999

#82
Burrito Company
Cuisines: American, Mexican
Average price: Modest
Address: Baaderstr. 68 80469 Munich
Phone: +49 89 21965986

#83
Sushi Cent
Cuisines: Sushi Bar
Average price: Expensive
Address: Schneckenburgerstr. 31 81675 Munich
Phone: +49 89 475834

#84
Restaurant Osteria Mugolone
Cuisines: Italian
Average price: Expensive
Address: Maillingerstr. 12 80636 Munich
Phone: +49 89 12739836

#85
Arkadas Kebap Haus
Cuisines: Kebab
Average price: Modest
Address: Wendl-Dietrich-Str. 17 80634 Munich
Phone: +49 89 14330584

#86
Osteria Veneta
Cuisines: Italian, Pizza
Average price: Expensive
Address: Utzschneiderstr. 4 80469 Munich
Phone: +49 89 26022093

#87
Weinhaus Neuner
Cuisines: Wine Bar, Seafood, German
Average price: Expensive
Address: Herzogspitalstr. 8 80331 Munich
Phone: +49 89 2603954

#88
Munich72 Park
Cuisines: Beer Garden, Bar, Barbeque
Average price: Modest
Address: Kolehmainenweg 80809 Munich
Phone: +49 89 37691400

#89
Friulana
Cuisines: Italian
Average price: Modest
Address: Zenettistr. 43 80337 Munich
Phone: +49 89 766709

#90
Lohengrins Wirtshaus und Bar
Cuisines: German, Bavarian
Average price: Modest
Address: Cosimastr. 97 81925 Munich
Phone: +49 89 95927424

#91
SUSHIYA sansaro
Cuisines: Sushi Bar, Japanese
Average price: Expensive
Address: Amalienstr. 89 80799 Munich
Phone: +49 89 28808442

#92
Einstein
Cuisines: Middle Eastern, Israeli, Kosher
Average price: Expensive
Address: St.-Jakobs-Platz 18 80331 Munich
Phone: +49 89 202400332

#93
Nguyen
Cuisines: Vietnamese
Average price: Expensive
Address: Georgenstr. 67 80799 Munich
Phone: +49 89 28803451

#94
Gaststätte Königsquelle
Cuisines: Gastropub
Average price: Modest
Address: Baaderplatz 2 80469 Munich
Phone: +49 89 220071

#95
Ionion
Cuisines: Fast Food, Greek, Barbeque
Average price: Inexpensive
Address: Augustenstr. 90 80798 Munich
Phone: +49 89 5234552

#96
Sushi Sano
Cuisines: Sushi Bar
Average price: Inexpensive
Address: Josephspitalstr. 4 80331 Munich
Phone: +49 89 267490

Munich Restaurant Guide 2018 / Restaurants, Bars & Cafés

#97
Barer 61
Cuisines: Café
Average price: Modest
Address: Barer Str. 61 80799 Munich
Phone: +49 89 32602496

#98
Schweiger2
Cuisines: Bar, European
Average price: Exclusive
Address: Lilienstr. 6 81669 Munich
Phone: +49 89 44429082

#99
Palau
Cuisines: German, Spanish, Sandwiches
Average price: Inexpensive
Address: Thalkirchner Str. 16 80337 Munich
Phone: +49 177 2385672

#100
Block House
Cuisines: Steakhouse
Average price: Expensive
Address: Leopoldstr.32 80802 Munich
Phone: +49 89 331718

#101
L'Angolo Della Pizza
Cuisines: Italian, Pizza
Average price: Modest
Address: Breisacherstr. 30 81667 Munich
Phone: +49 89 4488979

#102
Hofbräukeller
Cuisines: Bavarian, Beer Garden
Average price: Modest
Address: Innere Wienerstr. 19 81667 Munich
Phone: +49 89 4599250

#103
Bratwurst Glöckl am Dom
Cuisines: German
Average price: Modest
Address: Frauenplatz 9 80331 Munich
Phone: +49 89 2919450

#104
Andy's Krablergarten
Cuisines: German
Average price: Modest
Address: Thalkirchner Str. 2 80337 Munich
Phone: +49 89 26019148

#105
Caffé Fausto
Cuisines: Café
Average price: Modest
Address: Birkenleiten 41 81543 Munich
Phone: +49 89 62231113

#106
peony lounge
Cuisines: Asian Fusion, Lounge
Average price: Modest
Address: Hörwarthstr.4 80804 Munich
Phone: +49 89 30669891

#107
Pfistermühle
Cuisines: Bavarian
Average price: Expensive
Address: Pfisterstr. 4 80331 Munich
Phone: +49 89 23703865

#108
KVR Kapitales vom Rind
Cuisines: Bavarian, Steakhouse
Average price: Expensive
Address: Viktoriastr. 23 80803 Munich
Phone: +49 89 44237736

#109
Wirtshaus-Ridler
Cuisines: Bavarian, Brewerie
Average price: Modest
Address: Gollierstr. 83 80339 Munich
Phone: +49 89 72609733

#110
Steinheil 16
Cuisines: German
Average price: Modest
Address: Steinheilstr. 16 80333 Munich
Phone: +49 89 527488

#111
Café Neuhauser
Cuisines: Bar, Café, Pizza
Average price: Modest
Address: Schulstr. 28 80634 Munich
Phone: +49 89 20208857

#112
Pizzeria Grano
Cuisines: Pizza
Average price: Modest
Address: Sebastiansplatz 3 80331 Munich
Phone: +49 89 23269939

#113
Satyam
Cuisines: Indian
Average price: Modest
Address: Berg-am-laim-str.53 81673 Munich
Phone: +49 89 46096940

#114
Bratwurstherzl
Cuisines: German, Bavarian
Average price: Modest
Address: Dreifaltigkeitsplatz 1 80331 Munich
Phone: +49 89 295113

#115
Restaurant Toshi
Cuisines: Japanese, Sushi Bar
Average price: Exclusive
Address: Wurzerstr. 18 80539 Munich
Phone: +49 89 25546942

#116
L'Ancora
Cuisines: Italian, Pizza
Average price: Modest
Address: Schleißheimer Str. 201 80809 Munich
Phone: +49 89 30762952

#117
Wirtshaus zur Brez'n
Cuisines: German, Bavarian
Average price: Modest
Address: Leopoldstr. 72 80802 Munich
Phone: +49 89 390092

#118
Quan Com
Cuisines: Vietnamese
Average price: Modest
Address: Wendl-Dietrich-Str. 4 80634 Munich
Phone: +49 89 12022167

#119
Restaurant La Casina
Cuisines: Italian
Average price: Expensive
Address: Frohschammerstr. 14 80807 Munich
Phone: +49 89 3598320

#120
Taverna Naxos
Cuisines: Greek
Average price: Modest
Address: Verdistr. 33 81247 Munich
Phone: +49 89 85793920

#121
mangia e bevi
Cuisines: Italian, Pizza
Average price: Modest
Address: Balanstr. 47 81669 Munich
Phone: +49 89 44454504

#122
Tavernetta
Cuisines: Italian
Average price: Modest
Address: Hildegardstr. 9 80539 Munich
Phone: +49 89 21269426

#123
Dhaba
Cuisines: Indian
Average price: Modest
Address: Belgradstr. 16 80796 Munich
Phone: +49 89 38367771

#124
Joon
Cuisines: Café
Average price: Modest
Address: Theresienstr. 114 80333 Munich
Phone: +49 176 32239578

#125
Manouche
Cuisines: Lebanese, Vegan
Average price: Inexpensive
Address: Valleystr. 19 81371 Munich
Phone: +49 176 72162201

#126
Bavarese
Cuisines: Italian, German
Average price: Modest
Address: Ehrengutstr. 15 80469 Munich
Phone: +49 89 52033437

#127
Quattro Tavoli
Cuisines: Italian
Average price: Modest
Address: Dreimühlenstr. 10 80469 Munich
Phone: +49 89 74118157

#128
Gaststätte Großmarkthalle
Cuisines: German
Average price: Modest
Address: Kochelseestr. 13 81371 Munich
Phone: +49 89 764531

#129
Oleo Pazzo
Cuisines: Italian
Average price: Modest
Address: Schwanthalerstr. 37 80336 Munich
Phone: +49 89 54884882006

#130
Kim Sang - Panasia Cuisine
Cuisines: Asian Fusion, Japanese, Vietnamese
Average price: Modest
Address: Rosenkavalierplatz 15 81925 Munich
Phone: +49 89 99536996

#131
Conviva
Cuisines: German, European
Average price: Modest
Address: Hildegardstr. 1 80539 Munich
Phone: +49 89 23336977

#132
Bogenhauser Hof
Cuisines: German
Average price: Expensive
Address: Ismaninger Str. 85 81675 Munich
Phone: +49 89 985586

#133
Cafe Kosmos
Cuisines: Café, Lounge
Average price: Inexpensive
Address: Dachauer Str.7 80335 Munich
Phone: +49 175 3748756

#134
Burger House
Cuisines: Burgers
Average price: Modest
Address: Rablstr. 37 81667 Munich
Phone: +49 89 88903550

#135
Lemon Trees Thai
Cuisines: Thai, Beer Garden
Average price: Expensive
Address: Planeggerstr.9a 81241 Munich
Phone: +49 89 88952227

#136
Yee Chino Restaurant
Cuisines: Asian Fusion
Average price: Modest
Address: Helene-Weber-Allee 19 80637 Munich
Phone: +49 89 15988587

#137
Hechtsprung
Cuisines: European, Seafood, Mediterranean
Average price: Modest
Address: Homerstr. 3 80637 Munich
Phone: +49 89 15704930

#138
Biergarten am Viktualienmarkt
Cuisines: Bavarian, Beer Garden
Average price: Modest
Address: Viktualienmarkt 9 80331 Munich
Phone: +49 89 297545

#139
Laden
Cuisines: Café, Mediterranean, Breakfast & Brunch
Average price: Modest
Address: Türkenstr. 37 80799 Munich
Phone: +49 89 18904247

#140
Eclipse
Cuisines: Israeli, Kosher
Average price: Modest
Address: Heßstr. 51 80798 Munich
Phone: +49 89 522221

#141
Trattoria Bellini
Cuisines: Italian
Average price: Modest
Address: Nymphenburger Str. 98 80636 Munich
Phone: +49 89 12789888

#142
La Fattoria
Cuisines: Italian
Average price: Modest
Address: Schlotthauerstr. 16 81541 Munich
Phone: +49 89 62231496

#143
Burrito Company
Cuisines: American
Average price: Modest
Address: Augustenstr. 74 80333 Munich
Phone: +49 89 21965986

#144
Shandiz
Cuisines: Persian, Iranian
Average price: Modest
Address: Dachauerstr. 50 80335 Munich
Phone: +49 89 59947986

#145
Klinglwirt
Cuisines: Bavarian
Average price: Modest
Address: Balanstr. 16 81669 Munich
Phone: +49 89 85676199

#146
Hans Im Glück Burger Grill
Cuisines: Burgers
Average price: Modest
Address: Nymphenburger Str. 69 80335 Munich
Phone: +49 89 64299982

#147
NamGiao 31
Cuisines: Vietnamese
Average price: Modest
Address: Maistr. 31 80337 Munich
Phone: +49 89 59988033

#148
Piccola Italia
Cuisines: Italian, Pizza
Average price: Modest
Address: Aberlestr. 14 81371 Munich
Phone: +49 89 761844

#149
Last Supper
Cuisines: International, Lounge
Average price: Expensive
Address: Karlstr. 10 80333 Munich
Phone: +49 89 28808809

#150
Schnelle Liebe
Cuisines: Fast Food, European, Burgers
Average price: Modest
Address: Thalkirchnerstr. 12 80337 Munich
Phone: +49 89 21578752

#151
Halali
Cuisines: Restaurant
Average price: Exclusive
Address: Schönfeldstr. 22 80539 Munich
Phone: +49 89 285909

#152
Lago di Garda
Cuisines: Italian
Average price: Modest
Address: Baaderstr. 2 80469 Munich
Phone: +49 89 299144

#153
Rabiang Thai
Cuisines: Thai
Average price: Expensive
Address: Georgenschwaigstr. 25 80807 Munich
Phone: +49 89 3507304

#154
La Taquería
Cuisines: Mexican
Average price: Modest
Address: Zweibrückenstr. 9 80331 Munich
Phone: +49 89 55276787

#155
El Gusto
Cuisines: Café
Average price: Modest
Address: Amalienstr. 34 80799 Munich
Phone: +49 89 281281

#156
Esskapade
Cuisines: International
Average price: Modest
Address: Volkartstr. 70 80636 Munich
Phone: +49 89 20201838

#157
Tegernseer Tal Bräuhaus
Cuisines: Bavarian, German
Average price: Modest
Address: Im Tal 8 80331 Munich
Phone: +49 89 222626

#158
Königin 43
Cuisines: Café, Breakfast & Brunch
Average price: Modest
Address: Königinstr. 43 80539 Munich
Phone: +49 89 331262

#159
Malzraum
Cuisines: German, Bar
Average price: Modest
Address: Artilleriestr. 5 80636 Munich
Phone: +49 89 187997

#160
Bernard et Bernard
Cuisines: Crêperie
Average price: Modest
Address: Innere Wiener Str. 32 81667 Munich
Phone: +49 89 4801173

#161
Ristorante Limoni
Cuisines: Italian
Average price: Expensive
Address: Amalienstr. 38 80799 Munich
Phone: +49 89 28806029

#162
Blue Nile 1
Cuisines: African, Ethiopian
Average price: Modest
Address: Siegesstraße 22A 80802 Munich
Phone: +49 89 342389

#163
Brezelina
Cuisines: Fast Food, Specialty Food, Pretzels
Average price: Modest
Address: Karlsplatz 9 80335 Munich
Phone: +49 89 23540940

#164
Emporio Italiano
Cuisines: Italian, Delicatessen
Average price: Modest
Address: Volkartstr. 16 80634 Munich
Phone: +49 89 12555666

#165
Monte Grappa
Cuisines: Italian
Average price: Inexpensive
Address: Einsteinstr. 98 81675 Munich
Phone: +49 89 4703011

#166
Café Kitchenette
Cuisines: Coffee, Tea, Café
Average price: Modest
Address: Plinganserstr. 38a 81369 Munich
Phone: +49 89 74746299

#167
Merhaba
Cuisines: Turkish
Average price: Modest
Address: Pariser Str. 9 81669 Munich
Phone: +49 89 4487067

#168
Ninh
Cuisines: Asian Fusion, Oriental, Vietnamese
Average price: Inexpensive
Address: Alramstr. 27 81371 Munich
Phone: +49 89 76758448

#169
Perazzo
Cuisines: Italian
Average price: Exclusive
Address: Oskar-von-Miller-Ring 36 80333 Munich
Phone: +49 89 28986090

#170
The Caribbean Embassy
Cuisines: Caribbean, Cocktail Bar
Average price: Expensive
Address: Ganghoferstr. 68 80339 Munich
Phone: +49 89 54030610

#171
Potlatsch
Cuisines: German
Average price: Modest
Address: Agnes-Bernauer-Str. 98 80687 Munich
Phone: +49 89 58978191

#172
Zum Feinschmecker
Cuisines: German
Average price: Modest
Address: Kurfürstenplatz 3 80796 Munich
Phone: +49 89 2714149

#173
il Piccolo Principe
Cuisines: Italian
Average price: Modest
Address: Kapuzinerstr. 48 80469 Munich
Phone: +49 89 7213450

#174
Mystikon
Cuisines: Greek
Average price: Expensive
Address: Walchenseeplatz 4 81539 Munich
Phone: +49 89 62009339

#175
HaGuRuMa
Cuisines: Japanese
Average price: Modest
Address: Baaderstr. 62 80469 Munich
Phone: +49 89 2016911

#176
Kennedy's
Cuisines: Burgers, Irish Pub, Diner
Average price: Modest
Address: Sendlinger-Torplatz 11 80336 Munich
Phone: +49 89 59988460

#177
Asia Cuisine
Cuisines: Asian Fusion, Chinese
Average price: Inexpensive
Address: Buttermelcherstr. 2a 80469 Munich
Phone: +49 89 23889796

#178
Frenzy
Cuisines: European, Coffee, Tea, Lounge
Average price: Modest
Address: Fraunhoferstr. 20 80469 Munich
Phone: +49 89 20232686

#179
Cosmogrill
Cuisines: Burgers, Fast Food
Average price: Expensive
Address: Maximilianstr. 10 80539 Munich
Phone: +49 89 89059696

#180
Taverna del Sud
Cuisines: Italian, Pizza
Average price: Modest
Address: Widenmayerstr. 52 80538 Munich
Phone: +49 89 24292199

#181
Restaurant 181
Cuisines: German
Average price: Expensive
Address: Spiridon-Louis-Ring 7 80809 Munich
Phone: +49 89 350948181

#182
Osterwaldgarten
Cuisines: German, Beer Garden
Average price: Expensive
Address: Keferstr. 12 80802 Munich
Phone: +49 89 38405040

#183
Roecklplatz
Cuisines: European, Mediterranean, German
Average price: Modest
Address: Isartalstr. 26 80469 Munich
Phone: +49 89 45217129

#184
nonsolovino
Cuisines: Italian, Wine Bar
Average price: Modest
Address: Metzstr. 15 81667 Munich
Phone: +49 89 44499633

#185
Zum Kloster
Cuisines: Mediterranean, German
Average price: Modest
Address: Preysingstr. 77 81667 Munich
Phone: +49 89 4470564

#186
Il Trullo
Cuisines: Italian
Average price: Modest
Address: Albrechtstr. 32 80636 Munich
Phone: +49 89 18954192

#187
Lisboa Bar
Cuisines: Portuguese, Mediterranean, Bar
Average price: Modest
Address: Breisacherstr. 22 81667 Munich
Phone: +49 89 4482274

#188
Café Freiraum
Cuisines: Argentine
Average price: Modest
Address: Pestalozzistr. 8 80469 Munich
Phone: +49 89 2607749

#189
Fire Dragon
Cuisines: Chinese
Average price: Modest
Address: Paul-Heyse-Str. 29 80336 Munich
Phone: +49 89 59988466

#190
Solo Pizza
Cuisines: Italian, Pizza, Bar
Average price: Modest
Address: Bereiteranger 18 81541 Munich
Phone: +49 89 67972900

#191
Riva Tal
Cuisines: Pizza, Mediterranean
Average price: Modest
Address: Tal 44 80331 Munich
Phone: +49 89 220240

#192
Restaurant Myra
Cuisines: Bar, Turkish, Café
Average price: Modest
Address: Thalkirchner Str. 145 81371 Munich
Phone: +49 89 26018384

#193
Café Mozart
Cuisines: Coffee, Tea, Café, Bar
Average price: Modest
Address: Pettenkoferstr. 2 80336 Munich
Phone: +49 89 594190

#194
Restaurant Vinaiolo
Cuisines: Italian
Average price: Expensive
Address: Steinstr. 42 81667 Munich
Phone: +49 89 48950356

#195
Irodion
Cuisines: Greek
Average price: Modest
Address: Friedrich-Hebbel-Str. 18 81369 Munich
Phone: +49 89 7697365

#196
Swagat
Cuisines: Indian
Average price: Modest
Address: Prinzregentenplatz 13 81675 Munich
Phone: +49 89 47084844

#197
Spicery
Cuisines: Thai
Average price: Expensive
Address: Weißenburger Platz 3 81667 Munich
Phone: +49 89 67972680

#198
Wirtshaus Ayingers
Cuisines: German, Gastropub
Average price: Expensive
Address: Platzl 1A 80331 Munich
Phone: +49 89 23703666

#199
Nostos
Cuisines: Greek
Average price: Modest
Address: Blutenburgstr. 2 80636 Munich
Phone: +49 89 12027766

#200
Due Passi
Cuisines: Italian
Average price: Modest
Address: Ledererstr. 11 80331 Munich
Phone: +49 89 224271

#201
Hans im Glück
Cuisines: American, Burgers
Average price: Modest
Address: Türkenstr. 79 80799 Munich
Phone: +49 89 66664688

#202
Paulaner Bräuhaus
Cuisines: Bavarian
Average price: Modest
Address: Kapuzinerplatz 5 80337 Munich
Phone: +49 89 5446110

#203
La Corte dell Angelo
Cuisines: Italian
Average price: Expensive
Address: Perlacher Straße 11 81539 Munich
Phone: +49 89 62009640

#204
Nomiya
Cuisines: Japanese, German
Average price: Modest
Address: Wörthstr. 7 81667 Munich
Phone: +49 89 4484095

#205
Burger & Bier
Cuisines: Burgers, Bar
Average price: Modest
Address: Klenzestr. 40 80469 Munich
Phone: +49 89 72632644

#206
Dicke Sophie
Cuisines: German, Bavarian, Beer Garden
Average price: Modest
Address: Johanneskirchner Str. 146 81929 Munich
Phone: +49 89 95953634

#207
Kaisergarten
Cuisines: German, Bavarian, Beer Garden
Average price: Expensive
Address: Kaiserstr. 34 80801 Munich
Phone: +49 89 34020203

#208
Ganga
Cuisines: Indian
Average price: Modest
Address: Baaderstr. 11 80469 Munich
Phone: +49 89 2016465

#209
käppchen Burgergrill
Cuisines: Burgers, American
Average price: Modest
Address: Lindwurmstr.139a 80337 Munich
Phone: +49 89 41144273

#210
De Afric
Cuisines: African, Ethiopian
Average price: Modest
Address: Theresienstr. 146 80333 Munich
Phone: +49 89 23545039

#211
Bar Tapas Teatro
Cuisines: Spanish, Tapas Bar
Average price: Modest
Address: Balanstr. 23 81669 Munich
Phone: +49 89 48004284

#212
Forum
Cuisines: European, Bar, Breakfast & Brunch
Average price: Modest
Address: Corneliusstr. 2 80469 Munich
Phone: +49 89 268818

#213
Burger House 2
Cuisines: Burgers, Steakhouse, American
Average price: Modest
Address: Ismaninger Str. 5 81667 Munich
Phone: +49 89 92586552

#214
Tonkin
Cuisines: Vietnamese
Average price: Modest
Address: Lindwurmstr. 65 80337 Munich
Phone: +49 89 55879879

#215
Zum Steg
Cuisines: German
Average price: Inexpensive
Address: Dachauer Str. 29 80335 Munich
Phone: +49 89 54506724

#216
Ristorante alta marea
Cuisines: Italian, Seafood, Mediterranean
Average price: Modest
Address: Schönfeldstr. 15a 80539 Munich
Phone: +49 89 285357

#217
Restaurant Poseidon
Cuisines: Greek
Average price: Modest
Address: Leonrodstr. 85 80636 Munich
Phone: +49 89 18979623

#218
Gaststätte Stragula
Cuisines: Dive Bar, Gastropub
Average price: Modest
Address: Bergmannstr. 66 80339 Munich
Phone: +49 89 507743

#219
Pepenero Ristorante
Cuisines: Italian
Average price: Inexpensive
Address: Feilitzschstr. 23 80802 Munich
Phone: +49 89 38998883

#220
Chef In the City
Cuisines: Café
Average price: Expensive
Address: Fraunbergstr. 7 81379 Munich
Phone: +49 89 99940377

#221
GOA
Cuisines: Indian
Average price: Modest
Address: Thierschstr. 8 80538 Munich
Phone: +49 89 21111789

#222
Pizzesco
Cuisines: Pizza, Italian
Average price: Modest
Address: Rosenheimer Str. 12 81669 Munich
Phone: +49 89 67972812

#223
Spanoulis Alexis Sorbas
Cuisines: Greek
Average price: Modest
Address: Senftenauerstr. 187 80689 Munich
Phone: +49 89 57956930

#224
Österia
Cuisines: Austrian, Wine Bar
Average price: Modest
Address: Taubenstr. 2 81541 Munich
Phone: +49 89 62489924

#225
Cafe Cord
Cuisines: Bar, Café
Average price: Modest
Address: Sonnenstr. 19 80331 Munich
Phone: +49 89 54540780

#226
Hacienda
Cuisines: Mexican, Cocktail Bar
Average price: Modest
Address: Steinstr. 83 81667 Munich
Phone: +49 89 48998808

#227
Kreiller's
Cuisines: Café, International, Breakfast & Brunch
Average price: Modest
Address: Kreillerstr. 21 81673 Munich
Phone: +49 89 45458333

#228
CyClo
Cuisines: Asian Fusion, Vietnamese
Average price: Expensive
Address: Theresienstr. 70 80333 Munich
Phone: +49 89 28808390

#229
VUE Maximilian
Cuisines: German
Average price: Exclusive
Address: Maximilianstr. 17, 80539 80539 Munich
Phone: +49 89 21250

#230
Pietro Cannova
Cuisines: Delicatessen, Bistros
Average price: Inexpensive
Address: Tegernseer Landstr. 115 81539 Munich
Phone: +49 89 6923650

#231
Indian Mango
Cuisines: Indian
Average price: Inexpensive
Address: Zweibrückenstr. 15 80331 Munich
Phone: +49 89 25542424

#232
Biergarten Muffathalle
Cuisines: Beer Garden
Average price: Modest
Address: Zellstr. 4 81667 Munich
Phone: +49 89 45875073

#233
Cafe Vorhoelzer Forum der Fakultät für Architektur TUM
Cuisines: Café
Average price: Modest
Address: Arcisstr. 21 80333 Munich
Phone: +49 174 9748447

#234
Aumeister
Cuisines: German, Bavarian, Beer Garden
Average price: Modest
Address: Sondermeierstr. 1 80939 Munich
Phone: +49 89 18931420

#235
Il Grappolo
Cuisines: Italian
Average price: Modest
Address: Adalbertstr. 28 80799 Munich
Phone: +49 89 396241

#236
Taverna Kymata
Cuisines: Greek
Average price: Modest
Address: Volpinistr. 19 80638 Munich
Phone: +49 89 14332533

#237
Bobby's
Cuisines: Pizza, Italian
Average price: Modest
Address: Augustenstr. 62 80333 Munich
Phone: +49 89 66651731

#238
Augustiner am Platzl
Cuisines: German
Average price: Modest
Address: Münzstr. 8 80331 Munich
Phone: +49 89 2111356

#239
Lezizel Manti
Cuisines: Bistros, Turkish
Average price: Inexpensive
Address: Corneliusstr.6 80469 Munich
Phone: +49 162 2859535

#240
Keko
Cuisines: Turkish
Average price: Modest
Address: Mariahilfstraße 24 81541 Munich
Phone: +49 89 659969

#241
Centro Español
Cuisines: Spanish
Average price: Modest
Address: Daiserstr. 20 81371 Munich
Phone: +49 89 763653

#242
Schneewittchen am Glockenbach
Cuisines: Café
Average price: Modest
Address: Am Glockenbach 8 80469 Munich
Phone: +49 89 38904059

#243
Osaka Haus
Cuisines: Chinese, Sushi Bar
Average price: Inexpensive
Address: Augustenstr. 16 80333 Munich
Phone: +49 89 59068054

#244
Barista
Cuisines: Lounge, Restaurant
Average price: Expensive
Address: Kardinal-Faulhaber-Str 11 80333 Munich
Phone: +49 89 20802180

#245
Ecco Restaurant
Cuisines: Italian
Average price: Modest
Address: Kazmairstr. 47 80339 Munich
Phone: +49 89 99017979

#246
Georgios Taverne
Cuisines: Greek
Average price: Modest
Address: Schleißheimer Str. 188 80797 Munich
Phone: +49 89 3089396

#247
Osteria Italiana
Cuisines: Italian
Average price: Expensive
Address: Schellingstr. 62 80799 Munich
Phone: +49 89 2720717

#248
Wiesengrund
Cuisines: German, International
Average price: Modest
Address: Elsässer Str. 22 81667 Munich
Phone: +49 89 4489450

#249
Nefeli
Cuisines: Greek
Average price: Expensive
Address: Berger-Kreuz-Str. 26 81735 Munich
Phone: +49 89 45080269

#250
Restaurant Sankt Emmeramsmühle
Cuisines: German, Beer Garden
Average price: Expensive
Address: St. Emmeram 41 81925 Munich
Phone: +49 89 953971

#251
Rosso
Cuisines: Pizza
Average price: Modest
Address: Kapuzinerstr. 6 80337 Munich
Phone: +49 89 76701545

#252
Hoover & Floyd
Cuisines: Dive Bar, Bistros
Average price: Modest
Address: Ickstattstr. 2 80469 Munich
Phone: +49 89 26949015

#253
Apostel's
Cuisines: Greek
Average price: Modest
Address: Schweigerstr. 10 81541 Munich
Phone: +49 89 67972740

#254
Die Neue Fasanerie
Cuisines: German, Beer Garden, International
Average price: Expensive
Address: Hartmannshoferstr 20 80997 Munich
Phone: +49 89 1495607

#255
Theresa
Cuisines: Seafood, Steakhouse
Average price: Expensive
Address: Theresienstr. 29 80333 Munich
Phone: +49 89 28803301

#256
Blu Mediteraneo
Cuisines: Mediterranean, Seafood, Winery
Average price: Expensive
Address: Bauerstr. 2 80796 Munich
Phone: +49 89 27312288

#257
L'Amar
Cuisines: Mediterranean, Café
Average price: Modest
Address: Pestalozzistr. 28 80469 Munich
Phone: +49 89 54892327

#258
GURU
Cuisines: Indian, Pakistani
Average price: Modest
Address: Wasserburger Landstr. 204a 81827 Munich
Phone: +49 89 43777227

#259
Le Cezanne
Cuisines: French
Average price: Expensive
Address: Konradstr. 1 80801 Munich
Phone: +49 89 391805

#260
Zen
Cuisines: Asian Fusion
Average price: Expensive
Address: Arabellastr. 6 81925 Munich
Phone: +49 89 92640

#261
CA-BA-LU
Cuisines: Bar, Burgers
Average price: Modest
Address: Thierschplatz 5 80538 Munich
Phone: +49 89 94508840

#262
Alter Simpl
Cuisines: German
Average price: Modest
Address: Türkenstr. 57 80799 Munich
Phone: +49 89 2723083

#263
Bonjour Vietnam
Cuisines: Vietnamese
Average price: Modest
Address: Fallmerayerstr. 28 80796 Munich
Phone: +49 89 28788978

#264
Taverne Lithos
Cuisines: Greek
Average price: Inexpensive
Address: Wendelsteinstr. 11 81541 Munich
Phone: +49 89 694236

#265
Gratitude - organic eatery
Cuisines: Vegan
Average price: Modest
Address: Türkenstr. 55 80799 Munich
Phone: +49 89 88982174

#266
Deutsche Eiche
Cuisines: Hotel, German
Average price: Modest
Address: Reichenbachstr. 13 80469 Munich
Phone: +49 89 2311660

#267
Restaurant Al Paladino
Cuisines: Italian
Average price: Modest
Address: Heimeranplatz 1 80339 Munich
Phone: +49 89 5025657

#268
Sushi & Nudel Fuji
Cuisines: Japanese, Chinese, Sushi Bar
Average price: Inexpensive
Address: Nymphenburger Str.151 80634 Munich
Phone: +49 89 13010183

#269
The Victorian House - Brown's
Cuisines: Café, Pub
Average price: Expensive
Address: Türkenstr. 60 80799 Munich
Phone: +49 89 25543839

#270
Osteria Baal
Cuisines: Italian, Tapas Bar, Tapas
Average price: Modest
Address: Kreittmayrstr. 26 80335 Munich
Phone: +49 89 18703836

#271
L'Osteria
Cuisines: Pizza, Italian
Average price: Modest
Address: Leopoldstr. 28a 80802 Munich
Phone: +49 89 38889711

#272
Rive Gauche
Cuisines: French
Average price: Modest
Address: Thalkirchner Str. 11 80337 Munich
Phone: +49 89 23231898

#273
Wirtshaus Zamdorfer
Cuisines: Beer Garden, Gastropub
Average price: Modest
Address: Schwarzwaldstr. 2a 81677 Munich
Phone: +49 89 916921

#274
Lezizel Manti
Cuisines: Bistros, Turkish
Average price: Inexpensive
Address: Thalkirchner Str. 129 81371 Munich
Phone: +49 89 76703733

#275
Herrmannsdorfer Bistro
Cuisines: Bistros, Organic Store
Average price: Expensive
Address: Frauenstr. 6 80469 Munich
Phone: +49 89 263525

#276
Baricentro
Cuisines: Italian
Average price: Modest
Address: Sebastiansplatz 5 80331 Munich
Phone: +49 89 23259980

#277
Königlicher Hirschgarten
Cuisines: German, Beer Garden
Average price: Modest
Address: Hirschgartenallee 1 80639 Munich
Phone: +49 89 17999119

#278
An Nam
Cuisines: Vietnamese
Average price: Modest
Address: Pestalozzistr. 32 80469 Munich
Phone: +49 89 24203499

#279
Café im Hinterhof
Cuisines: International, Breakfast & Brunch
Average price: Modest
Address: Sedanstr. 29 81667 Munich
Phone: +49 89 4489964

#280
Pfälzer Residenz Weinstube
Cuisines: German, Bavarian, Gastropub
Average price: Modest
Address: Residenzstr. 1 80333 Munich
Phone: +49 89 225628

#281
Les Deux
Cuisines: French
Average price: Expensive
Address: Maffeistr. 3a 80333 Munich
Phone: +49 89 710407373

#282
Il Gambero
Cuisines: Italian
Average price: Modest
Address: Netzerstr. 29 80992 Munich
Phone: +49 89 142134

#283
Galerie Café Käthe
Cuisines: Coffee, Tea, Café
Average price: Modest
Address: Gebsattelstr. 34 81541 Munich
Phone: +49 179 7805363

#284
El Patio
Cuisines: Bar, Mexican
Average price: Modest
Address: Herzogstr. 88 80796 Munich
Phone: +49 89 32388586

#285
NI HAO
Cuisines: Chinese
Average price: Inexpensive
Address: Amalienstr. 45 80799 Munich
Phone: +49 89 88981668

#286
bon valeur
Cuisines: European
Average price: Modest
Address: Sonnenstr. 17 80331 Munich
Phone: +49 89 54883994

#287
Vegelangelo
Cuisines: Vegetarian
Average price: Expensive
Address: Thomas-Wimmer-Ring 16 80538 Munich
Phone: +49 89 28806836

#288
Michaeligarten
Cuisines: German, Beer Garden
Average price: Modest
Address: Feichtstr. 10 81735 Munich
Phone: +49 89 43552424

Munich Restaurant Guide 2018 / Restaurants, Bars & Cafés

#289
Phong Phu
Cuisines: Chinese, Asian Fusion
Average price: Inexpensive
Address: An Der Hauptfeuerwache 12 80331 Munich
Phone: +49 89 12280398

#290
Kam Lung
Cuisines: Chinese
Average price: Modest
Address: Blutenburgstr. 53 80636 Munich
Phone: +49 89 1291254

#291
Metronom
Cuisines: Greek, Bar
Average price: Modest
Address: Bruderhofstr. 5 81371 Munich
Phone: +49 178 4771079

#292
Bistro Pho 79
Cuisines: Vietnamese
Average price: Inexpensive
Address: Theresienstr. 79 80333 Munich
Phone: +49 89 15883479

#293
MAN FAT
Cuisines: Chinese
Average price: Modest
Address: Barerstr. 53 80799 Munich
Phone: +49 89 2720962

#294
Gaststätte Liebighof
Cuisines: German, Bavarian
Average price: Modest
Address: Liebigstr. 14 80538 Munich
Phone: +49 89 295405

#295
Gaststätte Osteria da Antonio
Cuisines: Italian
Average price: Modest
Address: Fasaneriestr. 4 80636 Munich
Phone: +49 89 1231265

#296
Arts n' Boards
Cuisines: International, Bar, Breakfast & Brunch
Average price: Modest
Address: Belgradstr. 9 80796 Munich
Phone: +49 89 30658490

#297
Kerala
Cuisines: Indian
Average price: Modest
Address: Schumannstr. 9 81679 Munich
Phone: +49 89 41200548

#298
Birreria e Trattoria Seerose
Cuisines: Italian
Average price: Expensive
Address: Feilitzschstr. 32 80802 Munich
Phone: +49 89 461331420

#299
Vietha
Cuisines: Vietnamese, Thai, Vegetarian
Average price: Modest
Address: Landsbergerstr 104 80339 Munich
Phone: +49 89 51878869

#300
Café Neuhausen
Cuisines: European, Lounge, Café, Coffee, Tea
Average price: Modest
Address: Blutenburgstr 106 80636 Munich
Phone: +49 89 18975570

#301
Italy
Cuisines: Italian
Average price: Modest
Address: Leopoldstr. 108 80802 Munich
Phone: +49 89 346403

#302
Westend
Cuisines: Bar, Café, Coffee, Tea
Average price: Modest
Address: Anglerstr. 32 80339 Munich
Phone: +49 89 508341

#303
Joe Pena's
Cuisines: Mexican, Cocktail Bar
Average price: Modest
Address: Buttermelcherstr. 17 80469 Munich
Phone: +49 89 226463

#304
Sushiya Bento
Cuisines: Japanese, Sushi Bar
Average price: Modest
Address: Lindwurmstr. 108 80337 Munich
Phone: +49 89 7411855588

#305
Thang Long
Cuisines: Vietnamese, Delicatessen
Average price: Inexpensive
Address: Poccistr 2 80336 Munich
Phone: +49 89 78071878

#306
Gerners
Cuisines: Bar, Beer Garden, German
Average price: Modest
Address: Dantestr. 33 80637 Munich
Phone: +49 89 15925174

#307
Blücher
Cuisines: German
Average price: Modest
Address: Keferloherstr. 87 80807 Munich
Phone: +49 89 35009188

#308
Mangostin Asia
Cuisines: Asian Fusion
Average price: Expensive
Address: Maria-Einsiedelstr. 2 81379 Munich
Phone: +49 89 7232031

#309
Coccinella-Holzofenpizza
Cuisines: Pizza
Average price: Modest
Address: Dachauer Str. 38 80335 Munich
Phone: +49 89 59943990

#310
Konditorei Widmann
Cuisines: Café, Chocolate Shop, Patisserie/Cake Shop
Average price: Expensive
Address: Heiglhofstr. 11 81377 Munich
Phone: +49 89 7146409

#311
Marais
Cuisines: Café
Average price: Modest
Address: Parkstr. 2 80339 Munich
Phone: +49 89 50094552

#312
Mai
Cuisines: Vietnamese
Average price: Modest
Address: Klenzestr. 8 80469 Munich
Phone: +49 89 2283303

#313
Sushi-Sano
Cuisines: Chinese, Sushi Bar
Average price: Inexpensive
Address: Zweibrückenstr. 19 80331 Munich
Phone: +49 89 21568330

#314
Nhu-Y
Cuisines: Vietnamese, Vegetarian, Asian Fusion
Average price: Modest
Address: Leonrodstr. 27 80636 Munich
Phone: +49 89 1238925

#315
Gaststätte Lindwurmstüberl
Cuisines: German, Bavarian, Gastropub
Average price: Modest
Address: Lindwurmstr. 32 80337 Munich
Phone: +49 89 53886531

#316
Wirtshaus Zur Marienburg
Cuisines: Gastropub
Average price: Modest
Address: Hohensalzaer Str. 1 81929 Munich
Phone: +49 89 93932239

#317
Cafe Glockenspiel
Cuisines: Wine Bar, Café
Average price: Expensive
Address: Marienplatz 28 80331 Munich
Phone: +49 89 264256

#318
El Gordo Loco
Cuisines: Mexican
Average price: Modest
Address: Mariannenstr. 3 80538 Munich
Phone: +49 89 21268355

#319
Bodega Dali
Cuisines: Wine Bar, Tapas, Tapas Bar
Average price: Modest
Address: Tengstr. 6 80798 Munich
Phone: +49 89 27779696

#320
Restaurant Il Dottore
Cuisines: Italian
Average price: Modest
Address: Pettenkoferstr. 1 80336 Munich
Phone: +49 89 54541954

#321
Pureburrito
Cuisines: Mexican
Average price: Modest
Address: Lindwurmstr. 57 80337 Munich
Phone: +49 89 59043711

#322
Lotus Asia Imbiss
Cuisines: Specialty Food, Fast Food
Average price: Inexpensive
Address: Hofmannstr.30 81379 Munich
Phone: +49 89 78019626

#323
Amber
Cuisines: Indian
Average price: Modest
Address: Ostpreußen str. 45 81927 Munich
Phone: +49 89 99939775

#324
Dilan Meze & Bar
Cuisines: Turkish
Average price: Modest
Address: Gebsattelstr. 15 81541 Munich
Phone: +49 89 15900097

#325
Hanshe Restaurant
Cuisines: Chinese
Average price: Modest
Address: Leopoldstr. 173 80804 Munich
Phone: +49 89 36076989

#326
La Stanza
Cuisines: Bar, Italian, Breakfast & Brunch
Average price: Expensive
Address: St.-Anna-Str. 13 80538 Munich
Phone: +49 89 25542393

#327
Kleiner Ochs'nbrater
Cuisines: Fast Food, Bavarian, Beer Garden
Average price: Modest
Address: Viktualienmarkt 11 80331 Munich
Phone: +49 89 298282

#328
Würschtl Bude
Cuisines: Food Stand
Average price: Inexpensive
Address: Einsteinstr. 84 81675 Munich
Phone: +49 89 65113677

#329
Adesso
Cuisines: Italian, Pizza
Average price: Inexpensive
Address: Rotwandstr. 1 81541 Munich
Phone: +49 89 54788927

#330
Spatenhaus an der Oper
Cuisines: German, Bavarian
Average price: Expensive
Address: Residenzstr. 12 80333 Munich
Phone: +49 89 290706-0

#331
Sushi Magie
Cuisines: Sushi Bar, Asian Fusion
Average price: Modest
Address: Westenriederstr. 13 80331 Munich
Phone: +49 89 21668264

#332
Pâtisserie Café Dukatz
Cuisines: Café, Coffee, Tea
Average price: Modest
Address: St.-Anna-Str. 11 80538 Munich
Phone: +49 89 20062893

#333
TAJ MAHAL
Cuisines: Indian
Average price: Modest
Address: Nymphenburgerstr. 145
80636 Munich
Phone: +49 89 12007050

#334
Lucullus
Cuisines: Greek
Average price: Inexpensive
Address: Birkenau 31 81543 Munich
Phone: +49 89 662951

#335
Thanh's Asia-Feinkost
Cuisines: Asian Fusion
Average price: Inexpensive
Address: Schlörstr. 15 80634 Munich
Phone: +49 1301 0983

#336
Ksara
Cuisines: Lebanese
Average price: Expensive
Address: Haimhauserstr. 7 80802 Munich
Phone: +49 89 33088297

#337
Café Gegenüber
Cuisines: Café
Average price: Inexpensive
Address: Barer Str. 80 80799 Munich
Phone: +49 89 32602496

#338
Opatija
Cuisines: Mediterranean
Average price: Modest
Address: Hochbrückenstr. 3 80331 Munich
Phone: +49 89 268353

#339
Lucky Sushi
Cuisines: Sushi Bar, Wok
Average price: Inexpensive
Address: Theresienstr. 57 80333 Munich
Phone: +49 89 57004575

#340
Ocui
Cuisines: Italian, Asian Fusion
Average price: Modest
Address: Oberanger 31-33 80331 Munich
Phone: +49 89 45226001

#341
Trattoria Da Pino
Cuisines: Italian, Pizza
Average price: Modest
Address: Hohenzollernstr. 26 80801 Munich
Phone: +49 89 390778

#342
Dillinger Chicago Bar'n Grill
Cuisines: Burgers, Bar, American
Average price: Modest
Address: Hofmannstr. 19 81379 Munich
Phone: +49 89 78749010

#343
Koriander Too
Cuisines: Vietnamese
Average price: Expensive
Address: Einsteinstr. 113 81675 Munich
Phone: +49 89 45709107

#344
Zum Augustiner
Cuisines: German, Bavarian
Average price: Modest
Address: Neuhauserstr. 27 80331 Munich
Phone: +49 89 23183257

#345
Alba Trattoria
Cuisines: Italian
Average price: Expensive
Address: Oberföhringer Str. 44 81925 Munich
Phone: +49 89 985353

#346
Zimt & Koriander
Cuisines: Café, Breakfast & Brunch, Specialty Food
Average price: Modest
Address: Lerchenauer Str. 189 80935 Munich
Phone: +49 1522 8818276

#347
Chez-Philippe
Cuisines: French
Average price: Expensive
Address: Zehentbauernstr. 20 81539 Munich
Phone: +49 89 18922233

#348
Redhot
Cuisines: Bar, American
Average price: Modest
Address: Amalienstr. 89 80799 Munich
Phone: +49 89 20061718

#349
Lotus Lounge
Cuisines: Thai
Average price: Modest
Address: Hans-Sachsstr. 10 80469 Munich
Phone: +49 89 21899755

#350
Wirtshaus Valley's
Cuisines: German
Average price: Modest
Address: Aberlestr. 52 81371 Munich
Phone: +49 89 76775151

#351
Truderinger Wirtshaus
Cuisines: Bavarian, Mediterranean, Beer Garden
Average price: Modest
Address: Kirchtruderinger Str. 17 81829 Munich
Phone: +49 89 421532

Munich Restaurant Guide 2018 / Restaurants, Bars & Cafés

#352
Schuhbecks in den Südtiroler Stuben
Cuisines: German
Average price: Exclusive
Address: Platzl 6-8 80331 Munich
Phone: +49 89 216690-0

#353
Restaurant Louis
Cuisines: French
Average price: Expensive
Address: Tattenbachstr. 1 80538 Munich
Phone: +49 89 44141910

#354
Görreshof
Cuisines: German, Bavarian, Beer Garden
Average price: Modest
Address: Görresstr. 38 80798 Munich
Phone: +49 89 20209550

#355
Julep's New York
Cuisines: Bar, Burgers, Mexican
Average price: Modest
Address: Breisacher Str. 18 81667 Munich
Phone: +49 89 4480044

#356
Poseidon
Cuisines: Greek
Average price: Modest
Address: Maria-Ward-Str. 24 80638 Munich
Phone: +49 89 17094466

#357
VolkArt
Cuisines: Tapas Bar, Mediterranean
Average price: Modest
Address: Volkartstr. 15 80634 Munich
Phone: +49 89 21969883

#358
Zum Flaucher
Cuisines: Beer Garden, German
Average price: Modest
Address: Isarauen 8 81379 Munich
Phone: +49 89 7232677

#359
Georgenhof
Cuisines: German
Average price: Modest
Address: Friedrichstr. 1 80801 Munich
Phone: +49 89 34077691

#360
Plaa Uan - Dicker Fisch
Cuisines: Thai
Average price: Expensive
Address: Theresienstr. 134 80333 Munich
Phone: +49 89 51877846

#361
Villa Toscana
Cuisines: Italian
Average price: Modest
Address: Bajuwarenstr. 131 81825 Munich
Phone: +49 89 422521

#362
Davvero
Cuisines: Mediterranean, Italian
Average price: Expensive
Address: Sophienstr. 28 80333 Munich
Phone: +49 89 5445551200

#363
Limani
Cuisines: Greek
Average price: Modest
Address: Rotdornstr. 2 81547 Munich
Phone: +49 89 69804072

#364
Aquamarina Espresso Bar
Cuisines: Italian, Café
Average price: Inexpensive
Address: Pappenheim Str. 3 80335 Munich
Phone: +49 89 55079990

#365
Café Wölfl
Cuisines: Bakery, Café
Average price: Modest
Address: Kellerstr. 17 81667 Munich
Phone: +49 89 481271

#366
White Rabbit's Room Kitchen & Store
Cuisines: Café
Average price: Modest
Address: Franziskanerstraße 19 81667 Munich
Phone: +49 89 67971193

#367
Phó - Flavour of Vietnam
Cuisines: Vietnamese, Wok
Average price: Inexpensive
Address: Nymphenburgerstr. 70 80335 Munich
Phone: +49 89 12738768

#368
Locanda Trevisana Ristorante
Cuisines: Italian
Average price: Modest
Address: Schulstr.41 80634 Munich
Phone: +49 89 20244404

#369
Taverna Anemos
Cuisines: Greek
Average price: Modest
Address: Willibaldstr.24 80689 Munich
Phone: +49 89 574448

#370
S'Maillinger
Cuisines: Bavarian, Austrian
Average price: Modest
Address: Maillinger Str. 4 80636 Munich
Phone: +49 89 78795888

#371
Munich 72
Cuisines: Dive Bar, Breakfast & Brunch, International
Average price: Modest
Address: Holzstr. 16 80469 Munich
Phone: +49 89 97343785

#372
Bento Ya
Cuisines: Japanese
Average price: Modest
Address: Augustenstr. 4 80333 Munich
Phone: +49 89 51556699

#373
Sappralott Gaststätten
Cuisines: Bar, German
Average price: Modest
Address: Donnersbergerstr. 37 80634 Munich
Phone: +49 89 164725

#374
Escobar
Cuisines: Tex-Mex, Cocktail Bar
Average price: Modest
Address: Breisacher Str. 19 81667 Munich
Phone: +49 89 485137

#375
Seehaus
Cuisines: Mediterranean, Beer Garden
Average price: Expensive
Address: Kleinhesselohe 3 80802 Munich
Phone: +49 89 3816130

#376
Briciole
Cuisines: Café
Average price: Modest
Address: Oskar-von-Miller-Ring 31 80333 Munich
Phone: +49 89 24242480

#377
Jin
Cuisines: Chinese
Average price: Exclusive
Address: Kanalstr. 14 80538 Munich
Phone: +49 89 21949970

#378
Santorini
Cuisines: Food, Greek
Average price: Modest
Address: Irschenhauserstr. 22 81379 Munich
Phone: +49 89 72496733

#379
Picnic
Cuisines: International, Vegan, Vegetarian
Average price: Modest
Address: Barer Str. 48 80799 Munich
Phone: +49 89 20061014

#380
Ohayou
Cuisines: Japanese, Sushi Bar
Average price: Modest
Address: Belgradstr.71 80804 Munich
Phone: +49 89 32667604

#381
Wirtshaus Sendlinger Augustiner
Cuisines: German
Average price: Modest
Address: Alramstr. 24 81371 Munich
Phone: +49 89 7470925

#382
vinpasa ristorante e bar
Cuisines: Italian
Average price: Expensive
Address: Isabellastr. 47 80796 Munich
Phone: +49 89 27373511

#383
Restaurant Hippocampus
Cuisines: Italian
Average price: Expensive
Address: Mühlbaurstr. 5 81677 Munich
Phone: +49 89 475855

#384
Hungriges Herz
Cuisines: Café, International
Average price: Modest
Address: Fraunhoferstr. 42 80469 Munich
Phone: +49 89 12073863

#385
Sitar
Cuisines: Indian
Average price: Modest
Address: Robert-Koch-Str. 4 80538 Munich
Phone: +49 89 21112361

#386
Poseidon
Cuisines: Greek
Average price: Modest
Address: Säbenerstr. 9 81547 Munich
Phone: +49 89 6921039

#387
Tafel & Schwafel
Cuisines: Coffee, Tea, Breakfast & Brunch
Average price: Modest
Address: Augustenstr. 80 80333 Munich
Phone: +49 89 45229522

#388
Cotidiano
Cuisines: Café, Breakfast & Brunch
Average price: Modest
Address: Gärtnerplatz 6 80469 Munich
Phone: +49 89 24207860

#389
La Trattoria
Cuisines: Italian, Wine Bar
Average price: Modest
Address: Lochhamer Str. 49 81477 Munich
Phone: +49 89 7856220

#390
Holy Burger
Cuisines: Burgers, Fast Food, Barbeque
Average price: Modest
Address: Wörthstr. 7 81667 Munich
Phone: +49 89 46229355

#391
Kaffeeladen & Espressobar
Cuisines: Café
Average price: Modest
Address: Donnersbergerstr. 55 80634 Munich
Phone: +49 176 38956459

#392
Blauer Bock
Cuisines: Bavarian, Bar
Average price: Exclusive
Address: Sebastiansplatz 9 80331 Munich
Phone: +49 89 45222333

#393
Taverna Lakis
Cuisines: Greek
Average price: Modest
Address: Augustenstr. 114 80798 Munich
Phone: +49 89 5233752

#394
Restaurant Schinken-Peter
Cuisines: German, Bavarian, Beer Garden
Average price: Modest
Address: Perlacher Str. 53 81539 Munich
Phone: +49 89 6973590

#395
Zum goldenen Kalb
Cuisines: Steakhouse
Average price: Exclusive
Address: Utzschneiderstr. 1 80469 Munich
Phone: +49 89 23542290

#396
Haxnbauer im Scholastikahaus
Cuisines: Bavarian
Average price: Expensive
Address: Sparkassenstr. 80331 Munich
Phone: +49 89 2166540

#397
Kreuzberger
Cuisines: German, Bar
Average price: Modest
Address: Westermühlstraße 32 80469 Munich
Phone: +49 89 20207287

#398
Wirtshaus Kurgarten
Cuisines: German, Gastropub
Average price: Modest
Address: De-la-Paz-Str. 10 80639 Munich
Phone: +49 89 17999081

#399
Nero
Cuisines: Pizza, Italian, Steakhouse
Average price: Expensive
Address: Rumfordstr. 34 80469 Munich
Phone: +49 89 21019060

#400
Brasserie Tresznjewski
Cuisines: Brasseries, International, Cocktail Bar
Average price: Modest
Address: Theresienstr. 72 80333 Munich
Phone: +49 89 282349

#401
pureburrito
Cuisines: Mexican, Fast Food
Average price: Modest
Address: Schellingstr. 104 80978 Munich
Phone: +49 89 51777805

#402
Restaurant Dalmatiner Grill
Cuisines: Serbo Croatian
Average price: Modest
Address: Geibelstr. 10 81679 Munich
Phone: +49 89 4704415

#403
Villa Dante
Cuisines: Italian
Average price: Modest
Address: Dantestr. 22 80637 Munich
Phone: +49 89 14346137

#404
The Potting Shed
Cuisines: Bar, Burgers, Tapas
Average price: Modest
Address: Occamstr. 11 80802 Munich
Phone: +49 89 34077284

#405
Augustiner Schützengarten
Cuisines: Bavarian, Beer Garden
Average price: Modest
Address: Zielstattstr. 6 81379 Munich
Phone: +49 89 72468088

#406
Restaurant Pils Corner
Cuisines: Restaurant
Average price: Modest
Address: Dachauerstraße 288 80992 Munich
Phone: +49 89 1407034

#407
Einfach & Gut
Cuisines: Italian
Average price: Modest
Address: Friedrichstr. 30 80801 Munich
Phone: +49 89 38879739

#408
Neuhauser Augustiner
Cuisines: German
Average price: Modest
Address: Hübnerstr. 23 80637 Munich
Phone: +49 89 1202130

#409
Brotraum
Cuisines: Bakery, Café
Average price: Modest
Address: Herzogstr. 6 80803 Munich
Phone: +49 89 761021

#410
Marietta Cucina
Cuisines: Italian
Average price: Modest
Address: Westendstr. 33 80339 Munich
Phone: +49 89 22849660

#411
Café Camera
Cuisines: Café, International
Average price: Inexpensive
Address: Schwanthalerstr. 88 80336 Munich
Phone: +49 4908 9536482

#412
LeDu | Happy Dumplings
Cuisines: Asian Fusion, Chinese
Average price: Modest
Address: Theresienstr. 18 80333 Munich
Phone: +49 89 95898460

#413
gennaro
Cuisines: Italian
Average price: Modest
Address: Fritz-Endress-Str. 4 81373 Munich
Phone: +49 89 74640775

#414
Insel-Mühle
Cuisines: German, Beer, Wine, Spirits, Bar, Hotel
Average price: Modest
Address: Von-Kahrstr. 87 80999 Munich
Phone: +49 89 81010

#415
Bachmaier-Hofbräu
Cuisines: Dive Bar, German
Average price: Modest
Address: Leopoldstr. 50 80802 Munich
Phone: +49 89 3838680

#416
Faun
Cuisines: European
Average price: Modest
Address: Hans-Sachs-Str. 17 80469 Munich
Phone: +49 89 263798

#417
Kushiage Enn
Cuisines: Japanese
Average price: Expensive
Address: Barer Straße 65 80799 Munich
Phone: +49 89 27372641

#418
Ratchada
Cuisines: Thai, Cocktail Bar
Average price: Modest
Address: Schwanthalerstr. 8 80336 Munich
Phone: +49 89 431785

#419
Le Florida
Cuisines: Bar, German
Average price: Modest
Address: Georgenstr. 48 80799 Munich
Phone: +49 89 44429555

#420
The Big Easy
Cuisines: Jazz, Blues, Cajun, Creole, American
Average price: Expensive
Address: Frundsbergstr. 46 80634 Munich
Phone: +49 89 15890253

#421
Klenze 17
Cuisines: Dive Bar, Burgers, German
Average price: Inexpensive
Address: Klenzestr. 17 80469 Munich
Phone: +49 89 2285795

#422
Le Faubourg
Cuisines: French
Average price: Expensive
Address: Kirchenstr. 5 81675 Munich
Phone: +49 89 475533

#423
Zum Koreaner
Cuisines: Korean
Average price: Inexpensive
Address: Amalienstr. 51 80799 Munich
Phone: +49 89 283115

#424
Ilios
Cuisines: Greek
Average price: Modest
Address: Situlistr. 7 80939 Munich
Phone: +49 89 36004112

#425
Van Hoa
Cuisines: Vietnamese
Average price: Modest
Address: Martin-Lutherstr. 8 81539 Munich
Phone: +49 89 62060880

#426
Speisezimmer
Cuisines: Gastropub
Average price: Modest
Address: Camerloherstrasse 82 80689 Munich
Phone: +49 89 56820360

#427
Makula
Cuisines: African
Average price: Modest
Address: Dreimühlenstr. 14 80469 Munich
Phone: +49 179 9422101

#428
Café Glück
Cuisines: Café, European
Average price: Modest
Address: Palmstraße 4 80469 Munich
Phone: +49 89 2011673

#429
Chopan am Gasteig
Cuisines: Afghan
Average price: Modest
Address: Rosenheimer Str. 6 81669 Munich
Phone: +49 89 44118571

#430
Happy Fildjan
Cuisines: Café, Coffee, Tea
Average price: Modest
Address: Gabelsbergerstr. 64 80333 Munich
Phone: +49 89 63851665

#431
Zum Ganghofer
Cuisines: Greek
Average price: Exclusive
Address: Ganghoferstr. 9 80339 Munich
Phone: +49 89 50096809

#432
Taklamakan
Cuisines: Food Stand
Average price: Modest
Address: Bayerstraße 27 80335 Munich
Phone: +49 89 54549878

#433
Deeba
Cuisines: Pakistani
Average price: Modest
Address: Barerstr. 42 80799 Munich
Phone: +49 89 283407

#434
Özdeveli
Cuisines: Turkish, Kebab
Average price: Modest
Address: Preysingstr. 2 81667 Munich
Phone: +49 89 48951798

#435
Bella Italia
Cuisines: Italian
Average price: Modest
Address: Weißenburgerstr. 2 81667 Munich
Phone: +49 89 486179

#436
La Bouche
Cuisines: French
Average price: Modest
Address: Jahnstr. 30 80469 Munich
Phone: +49 89 265626

#437
Bambushain
Cuisines: Asian Fusion, Vietnamese
Average price: Inexpensive
Address: Schleißheimerstr. 14 80333 Munich
Phone: +49 89 52314838

#438
Lehel
Cuisines: Cocktail Bar, Dance Club, German
Average price: Expensive
Address: Karl-Scharnagl-Ring 6-8 80538 Munich
Phone: +49 89 21111760

#439
Café Nymphenburg Sekt
Cuisines: Café, Coffee, Tea
Average price: Modest
Address: Viktualienmarkt Stand 5 80331 Munich
Phone: +49 89 23239660

#440
Jones
Cuisines: Diner, Burgers
Average price: Modest
Address: Karlstr. 56 80333 Munich
Phone: +49 89 54544777

#441
Café Schuntner
Cuisines: Café, Patisserie/Cake Shop
Average price: Modest
Address: Plinganserstr. 10 81369 Munich
Phone: +49 89 776393

#442
Essence
Cuisines: International, Lounge
Average price: Exclusive
Address: Gottfried-Keller-Str. 35 81245 Munich
Phone: +49 89 80040025

#443
La Bruschetta
Cuisines: Italian
Average price: Modest
Address: Nymphenburger Str. 53 80335 Munich
Phone: +49 89 1232442

#444
Ginger
Cuisines: Bar, Restaurant
Average price: Modest
Address: Augustenstr. 56 80333 Munich
Phone: +49 89 58989998

#445
Asia Bistro Minh
Cuisines: Chinese, Vietnamese
Average price: Inexpensive
Address: Amalienstr. 37 80799 Munich
Phone: +49 89 28779440

#446
Coco de Mer
Cuisines: International
Average price: Expensive
Address: Dreimühlenstr. 30 80469 Munich
Phone: +49 89 139276503

#447
Warmi Nudelbar
Cuisines: Japanese, Soup
Average price: Modest
Address: Barer Str. 56 80799 Munich
Phone: +49 89 95470016

#448
Pimay
Cuisines: Thai
Average price: Modest
Address: Barer Str. 68 80799 Munich
Phone: +49 89 24290655

#449
Bombay Tandoori
Cuisines: Indian
Average price: Inexpensive
Address: Rosenheimerstr. 75 81667 Munich
Phone: +49 89 44409422

#450
Luise Tagescafe
Cuisines: Café, Tapas
Average price: Inexpensive
Address: Luisenstr. 49 80333 Munich
Phone: +49 89 64299976

#451
Löwenbräukeller
Cuisines: German, Beer Garden
Average price: Modest
Address: Nymphenburgerstr. 2 80335 Munich
Phone: +49 89 54726690

#452
Taco Libre
Cuisines: Mexican, Fast Food
Average price: Modest
Address: Bahnhofplatz 5 80335 Munich
Phone: +49 89 55059393

#453
Obergiesinger
Cuisines: Austrian, Bavarian
Average price: Modest
Address: Bergstr. 5 81539 Munich
Phone: +49 89 55051666

#454
Pizzeria Da Bello e Bello
Cuisines: Pizza
Average price: Modest
Address: Elisabethstr. 19 80796 Munich
Phone: +49 89 27272034

#455
Cafe Haidhausen
Cuisines: Gastropub
Average price: Modest
Address: Franziskanerstr. 4 81669 Munich
Phone: +49 89 6886043

#456
Da Fausto
Cuisines: Italian
Average price: Expensive
Address: Helmtrudenstr 1 80805 Munich
Phone: +49 89 32705553

#457
Paulaner im Tal
Cuisines: German, Beer Garden
Average price: Modest
Address: Tal 12 80331 Munich
Phone: +49 89 219940-0

#458
La Ruota
Cuisines: Italian
Average price: Modest
Address: Landsberger Str. 428 81241 Munich
Phone: +49 89 836767

#459
Diyar Taverna
Cuisines: Turkish, Mediterranean
Average price: Modest
Address: Wörthstr. 10 81667 Munich
Phone: +49 89 48950497

#460
Manufactum brot&butter
Cuisines: Bakery, Food Delivery Services, Café
Average price: Modest
Address: Dienerstr. 12 80331 Munich
Phone: +49 89 23548250

#461
Emporio Armani Caffé Munich
Cuisines: Café
Average price: Expensive
Address: Theatinerstr. 12 80333 Munich
Phone: +49 89 5505280

#462
Locanda Busento
Cuisines: Italian
Average price: Modest
Address: Fürstenrieder Str. 277 81476 Munich
Phone: +49 89 78576070

#463
Leibspeis
Cuisines: German
Average price: Inexpensive
Address: Nymphenburgerstr. 105 80636 Munich
Phone: +49 89 18979677

#464
Attentat Griechischer Salat
Cuisines: Salad, European
Average price: Modest
Address: Zugspitzstr. 10 81541 Munich
Phone: +49 89 85635381

#465
Jammi - Asia
Cuisines: Asian Fusion, Vietnamese
Average price: Modest
Address: Schleißheimer Str. 69 80797 Munich
Phone: +49 89 44133235

#466
Viehhof Biergarten
Cuisines: Beer Garden
Average price: Modest
Address: Tumblingerstr. 29 80469 Munich
Phone: +49 89 6494360

#467
Das Edelweiß
Cuisines: German, European
Average price: Modest
Address: Edelweißstr. 10 81541 Munich
Phone: +49 89 64913780

#468
Austernkeller
Cuisines: Seafood
Average price: Exclusive
Address: Stollbergstr. 11 80539 Munich
Phone: +49 89 298787

#469
Café Altschwabing
Cuisines: Turkish, Gastropub, German
Average price: Modest
Address: Schellingstr. 56 80799 Munich
Phone: +49 89 2731022

#470
Ho Guom
Cuisines: Vietnamese, Thai
Average price: Modest
Address: Schleißheimer Str. 121 80797 Munich
Phone: +49 89 304257

#471
Trattoria Lindengarten
Cuisines: Italian
Average price: Expensive
Address: Agnes-Bernauer-Straßw 115 80687 Munich
Phone: +49 89 564452

#472
Kim's
Cuisines: Korean
Average price: Modest
Address: Theresienstr. 138 80333 Munich
Phone: +49 89 37966880

#473
Tattenbach
Cuisines: Bavarian
Average price: Modest
Address: Tattenbachstr. 6 80538 Munich
Phone: +49 89 225268

#474
Sesto Senso
Cuisines: Italian, Pizza
Average price: Modest
Address: Ohlmüllerstr. 12 81541 Munich
Phone: +49 89 62269330

#475
Asia Sushi Wok Express
Cuisines: Chinese, Japanese
Average price: Inexpensive
Address: Truderinger Str. 219 81825 Munich
Phone: +49 89 45665686

#476
China Restaurant Jade
Cuisines: Chinese, Asian Fusion
Average price: Modest
Address: Hofangerstr. 7 81735 Munich
Phone: +49 89 403124

#477
Il Falco
Cuisines: Italian
Average price: Inexpensive
Address: Falkenstr. 38 81541 Munich
Phone: +49 89 6515114

#478
La Fiera
Cuisines: Italian
Average price: Modest
Address: Heimeranstr. 57 80339 Munich
Phone: +49 89 503234

#479
Mai Garten
Cuisines: Chinese
Average price: Inexpensive
Address: Ohlmüllerstr. 24 81541 Munich
Phone: +49 89 62423888

#480
Caffè Ristretto
Cuisines: Italian, Specialty Food
Average price: Modest
Address: Kazmairstr. 30 80339 Munich
Phone: +49 89 74389403

#481
Le Stollberg
Cuisines: French
Average price: Expensive
Address: Stollbergstr. 2 80539 Munich
Phone: +49 89 24243450

#482
Trader Vic's
Cuisines: Pub, Lounge, German
Average price: Expensive
Address: Promenadeplatz 2-6 80333 Munich
Phone: +49 89 2120-0

#483
Marianne 'n' Hof Augustiner Bar
Cuisines: Bavarian
Average price: Modest
Address: Mariannenstr. 1 80538 Munich
Phone: +49 89 25544672

#484
casa d'angelo
Cuisines: Italian, Cocktail Bar
Average price: Modest
Address: Theo-Prosel-Weg 5 80797 Munich
Phone: +49 89 12713217

#485
Yak & Yeti Himalayan Food House
Cuisines: Himalayan/Nepalese
Average price: Modest
Address: Blücherstr. 1 80634 Munich
Phone: +49 89 16785838

#486
Los Faroles
Cuisines: Spanish
Average price: Modest
Address: Nordendstr. 26 80801 Munich
Phone: +49 89 89620076

#487
Schumann's Tagesbar
Cuisines: Bar, German
Average price: Expensive
Address: Maffeistr. 6 80333 Munich
Phone: +49 89 24217700

#488
P.Korn - Restaurant und Steaks
Cuisines: Steakhouse
Average price: Expensive
Address: Gabrielenstr.6 80636 Munich
Phone: +49 89 99930319

#489
Cannone Bar - Gola & Vino
Cuisines: Lounge, Italian
Average price: Modest
Address: Occamstr. 11 80802 Munich
Phone: +49 89 33035474

#490
Viva Maria
Cuisines: Italian, Bar, Pizza
Average price: Modest
Address: Rothmundstr. 5 80337 Munich
Phone: +49 89 535015

#491
Schweizer Hof
Cuisines: Gastropub, German
Average price: Inexpensive
Address: Planegger Str. 14 81241 Munich
Phone: +49 89 88184-0

#492
Taverna Avli
Cuisines: Greek
Average price: Modest
Address: Kreittmayrstr. 15 80335 Munich
Phone: +49 89 52059545

#493
Pini
Cuisines: Café, Bistros
Average price: Modest
Address: Klenzestr. 45 80469 Munich
Phone: +49 89 55274103

#494
Restaurant Hoa Quynh
Cuisines: Vietnamese, Thai
Average price: Modest
Address: Elsenheimerstr. 26 80687 Munich
Phone: +49 89 57877659

#495
Jordi´s Burrito
Cuisines: Mexican, Vegan, Vegetarian
Average price: Inexpensive
Address: Klenzestr. 16 80469 Munich
Phone: +49 89 38151917

#496
Scheidegger
Cuisines: German
Average price: Modest
Address: Bauerstr. 16 80796 Munich
Phone: +49 89 2714828

#497
Arte in Tavola
Cuisines: Italian, Mediterranean
Average price: Modest
Address: Schellingstr. 51 80799 Munich
Phone: +49 89 285136

#498
Nipponoodles
Cuisines: Japanese
Average price: Modest
Address: Gabelsbergerstr. 77 80333 Munich
Phone: +49 89 55261833

#499
Chopan
Cuisines: Afghan
Average price: Expensive
Address: Elvirastraße 18a 80636 Munich
Phone: +49 89 18956459

#500
fortuna cafébar
Cuisines: Coffee, Tea, Breakfast & Brunch
Average price: Modest
Address: Sedanstr. 18 81667 Munich
Phone: +49 89 18922823

Made in the USA
Middletown, DE
31 July 2018